MAP®

for the
Anxious Heart

BARBOUR
PUBLISHING

What Do Prayers for an Anxious Heart Look Like?...

Get ready to more fully experience the calming power of prayer in your everyday life with this creative journal...where every colorful page will guide you to create your very own prayer map—as you write out specific thoughts, ideas, and lists, which you can follow (from start to finish!)—as you talk to God. (Be sure to record the date on each one of your prayer maps so you can look back over time and see how God has continued to work in your life!)

The Prayer Map for the Anxious Heart will not only encourage you to spend time talking with God about the things that trouble your heart...it will also help you build a healthy spiritual habit of continual prayer for life!

Date:

Dear Heavenly Father,
....
....
....
....

Today, I am feeling anxious about. . .
....
....
....
....
....
....
....
....

I confess. . .
....
....
....
....
....
....
....
....

I trust that You will. . .
....
....
....
....
....

My soul needs. . .

I am grateful for. . .

Other things that I need to share
with You, God. . .

Amen. Thank You, Father, for hearing my prayers.

*Do not be anxious about anything, but in every
situation, by prayer and petition, with thanksgiving,
present your requests to God. And the peace of God,
which transcends all understanding, will guard
your hearts and your minds in Christ Jesus.*
PHILIPPIANS 4:6–7 NIV

Date:

Dear Heavenly Father,
....
....
....
....
....

Today, I am feeling anxious about. . .
....
....
....
....
....
....
....
....
....

I confess. . .
....
....
....
....
....
....
....
....
....

I trust that You will. . .
....
....
....
....
....

My soul needs. . .

I am grateful for. . .

Other things that I need to share with You, God. . .

Amen. Thank You, Father, for hearing my prayers.

"In GOD the LORD, we have an everlasting Rock."
ISAIAH 26:4 NASB

Date:

Dear Heavenly Father,

....
....
....
....

Today, I am feeling anxious about. . .

....
....
....
....
....
....
....
....

I confess. . .

....
....
....
....
....
....
....
....
....

I trust that You will. . .

....
....
....
....
....

My soul needs. . .

I am grateful for. . .

Other things that I need to share
with You, God. . .

Amen. Thank You, Father, for hearing my prayers.

*"Peace I leave with you; My peace I give to you;
not as the world gives do I give to you. Do not
let your heart be troubled, nor let it be fearful."*
JOHN 14:27 NASB

Date:

Dear Heavenly Father,

Today, I am feeling anxious about. . .

I confess. . .

I trust that You will. . .

My soul needs. . .

I am grateful for. . .

Other things that I need to share
with You, God. . .

Amen. Thank You, Father, for hearing my prayers.

_God arms me with strength,
and he makes my way perfect._
PSALM 18:32 NLT

Date:

Dear Heavenly Father,

I confess. . .

Today, I am feeling anxious about. . .

I trust that You will. . .

My soul needs. . .

I am grateful for. . .

Other things that I need to share
with You, God. . .

Amen. Thank You, Father, for hearing my prayers.

The righteous cry out, and the LORD hears them;
he delivers them from all their troubles.
PSALM 34:17 NIV

Date:

Dear Heavenly Father,

Today, I am feeling anxious about. . .

I confess. . .

I trust that You will. . .

My soul needs. . .

I am grateful for. . .

Other things that I need to share with You, God. . .

Amen. Thank You, Father, for hearing my prayers.

I will both lay me down in peace, and sleep:
for thou, LORD, only makest me dwell in safety.
PSALM 4:8 KJV

Date:

Dear Heavenly Father,

....
....
....
....

Today, I am feeling anxious about. . .

....
....
....
....
....
....
....
....

I confess. . .

....
....
....
....
....
....
....

I trust that You will. . .

....
....
....
....
....

My soul needs. . .

I am grateful for. . .

Other things that I need to share with You, God. . .

Amen. Thank You, Father, for hearing my prayers.

He is my God, and I trust him.
PSALM 91:2 NLT

Date:

Dear Heavenly Father,

Today, I am feeling anxious about. . .

I confess. . .

I trust that You will. . .

My soul needs. . .

I am grateful for. . .

Other things that I need to share with You, God. . .

Amen. Thank You, Father, for hearing my prayers.

*The LORD is close to the brokenhearted
and saves those who are crushed in spirit.*
PSALM 34:18 NIV

Date:

Dear Heavenly Father,
....
....
....
....
....

Today, I am feeling anxious about. . .
....
....
....
....
....
....
....
....
....
....
....

I confess. . .
....
....
....
....
....
....
....
....
....

I trust that You will. . .
....
....
....
....
....

My soul needs. . .

I am grateful for. . .

Other things that I need to share with You, God. . .

Amen. Thank You, Father, for hearing my prayers.

The Everlasting God, the LORD, the Creator of the ends of the earth does not become weary or tired.
ISAIAH 40:28 NASB

Date:

Dear Heavenly Father,

Today, I am feeling anxious about. . .

I confess. . .

I trust that You will. . .

My soul needs. . .

I am grateful for. . .

Other things that I need to share with You, God. . .

Amen. Thank You, Father, for hearing my prayers.

God is our refuge and strength,
a very present help in trouble.
PSALM 46:1 NASB

Date:

Dear Heavenly Father,
....
....
....
....

Today, I am feeling anxious about. . .
....
....
....
....
....
....
....
....
....
....

I confess. . .
....
....
....
....
....
....
....
....
....

I trust that You will. . .
....
....
....
....
....

My soul needs. . .

I am grateful for. . .

Other things that I need to share
with You, God. . .

Amen. Thank You, Father, for hearing my prayers.

*For You, Lord, are good, and ready
to forgive, and abundant in lovingkindness
to all who call upon You.*
PSALM 86:5 NASB

Date:

Dear Heavenly Father,..
....
....
....
....

Today, I am feeling anxious about. . .

I confess. . .

I trust that You will. . .

My soul needs. . .

I am grateful for. . .

Other things that I need to share
with You, God. . .

Amen. Thank You, Father, for hearing my prayers.

The righteous person may have many troubles,
but the LORD delivers him from them all.
PSALM 34:19 NIV

Date:

Dear Heavenly Father,

Today, I am feeling anxious about. . .

I confess. . .

I trust that You will. . .

My soul needs. . .

I am grateful for. . .

Other things that I need to share
with You, God. . .

Amen. Thank You, Father, for hearing my prayers.

*The Lord can be trusted to make you
strong and protect you from harm.*
2 Thessalonians 3:3 cev

Date:

Dear Heavenly Father, ...
....
....
....
....

Today, I am feeling anxious about. . .

....

I confess. . .

....

....

....

....

....

....

....

I trust that You will. . .

....
....
....
....
....

My soul needs. . .

I am grateful for. . .

Other things that I need to share with You, God. . .

Amen. Thank You, Father, for hearing my prayers.

*"The Lord will fight for you;
you need only to be still."*
Exodus 14:14 niv

Date:

Dear Heavenly Father,
....
....
....
....
....

Today, I am feeling anxious about. . .
....
....
....
....
....
....
....
....
....
....

I confess. . .
....
....
....
....
....
....
....
....

I trust that You will. . .
....
....
....
....
....

My soul needs. . .

I am grateful for. . .

Other things that I need to share with You, God. . .

Amen. Thank You, Father, for hearing my prayers.

Keep me as the apple of your eye;
hide me in the shadow of your wings.
PSALM 17:8 NIV

Date:

Dear Heavenly Father,

Today, I am feeling anxious about. . .

I confess. . .

I trust that You will. . .

My soul needs. . .

I am grateful for. . .

Other things that I need to share
with You, God. . .

Amen. Thank You, Father, for hearing my prayers.

I will wait for the God of my
salvation. My God will hear me.
MICAH 7:7 NASB

Date:

Dear Heavenly Father,..
....
....
....
....

Today, I am feeling anxious about. . .

....
....
....
....
....
....
....
....
....

I confess. . .

....
....
....
....
....
....
....
....

I trust that You will. . .

....
....
....
....
....

My soul needs. . .

I am grateful for. . .

Other things that I need to share
with You, God. . .

Amen. Thank You, Father, for hearing my prayers.

"Therefore I tell you, do not be anxious about
your life, what you will eat, nor about your
body, what you will put on. For life is more than
food, and the body more than clothing."
LUKE 12:22–23 ESV

Date:

Dear Heavenly Father,
....
....
....
....

Today, I am feeling anxious about. . .
....
....
....
....
....
....
....
....
....

I confess. . .
....
....
....
....
....
....
....
....
....

I trust that You will. . .
....
....
....
....
....

My soul needs. . .

I am grateful for. . .

Other things that I need to share
with You, God. . .

Amen. Thank You, Father, for hearing my prayers.

*"Do not worry about tomorrow,
for tomorrow will worry about itself.
Each day has enough trouble of its own."*
MATTHEW 6:34 NIV

Date:

Dear Heavenly Father,
....
....
....
....

Today, I am feeling anxious about. . .
....
....
....
....
....
....
....
....
....
....
....

I confess. . .
....
....
....
....
....
....
....
....
....

I trust that You will. . .
....
....
....
....
....

My soul needs. . .

I am grateful for. . .

Other things that I need to share
with You, God. . .

Amen. Thank You, Father, for hearing my prayers.

*Cast your cares on the Lord and he will sustain
you; he will never let the righteous be shaken.*
PSALM 55:22 NIV

Date:

Dear Heavenly Father,

Today, I am feeling anxious about. . .

I confess. . .

I trust that You will. . .

My soul needs. . .

I am grateful for. . .

Other things that I need to share
with You, God. . .

Amen. Thank You, Father, for hearing my prayers.

*"Don't be sad! This is a special day for the LORD,
and he will make you happy and strong."*
NEHEMIAH 8:10 CEV

Date:

Dear Heavenly Father,
....
....
....
....

Today, I am feeling anxious about. . .
....
....
....
....
....
....
....
....
....

I confess. . .
....
....
....
....
....
....
....
....
....

I trust that You will. . .
....
....
....
....
....

My soul needs. . .

I am grateful for. . .

Other things that I need to share
with You, God. . .

Amen. Thank You, Father, for hearing my prayers.

*"So do not fear; for I am with you; do not be dismayed,
for I am your God. I will strengthen you and help you;
I will uphold you with my righteous right hand."*
ISAIAH 41:10 NIV

Date:

Dear Heavenly Father,

Today, I am feeling anxious about. . .

I confess. . .

I trust that You will. . .

My soul needs. . .

I am grateful for. . .

Other things that I need to share with You, God. . .

Amen. Thank You, Father, for hearing my prayers.

Seek the LORD and his strength;
seek his presence continually!
PSALM 105:4 ESV

Date:

Dear Heavenly Father,

Today, I am feeling anxious about. . .

I confess. . .

I trust that You will. . .

My soul needs. . .

I am grateful for. . .

Other things that I need to share
with You, God. . .

Amen. Thank You, Father, for hearing my prayers.

*"Come to Me, all who are weary and
heavy-laden, and I will give you rest."*
MATTHEW 11:28 NASB

Date:

Dear Heavenly Father,
....
....
....
....
....

Today, I am feeling anxious about. . .
....
....
....
....
....
....
....
....
....
....

I confess. . .
....
....
....
....
....
....
....
....
....
....
....

I trust that You will. . .
....
....
....
....
....

My soul needs. . .

I am grateful for. . .

Other things that I need to share
with You, God. . .

Amen. Thank You, Father, for hearing my prayers.

Give all your worries and cares to God,
for he cares about you.
1 PETER 5:7 NLT

Date:

Dear Heavenly Father,
....
....
....
....

Today, I am feeling anxious about. . .
....
....
....
....
....
....
....
....
....
....

I confess. . .
....
....
....
....
....
....
....
....
....

I trust that You will. . .
....
....
....
....
....

My soul needs. . .

I am grateful for. . .

Other things that I need to share with You, God. . .

Amen. Thank You, Father, for hearing my prayers.

The LORD is my strength and my shield;
my heart trusts in him, and he helps me.
PSALM 28:7 NIV

Date:

Dear Heavenly Father,

Today, I am feeling anxious about...

I confess...

I trust that You will...

My soul needs. . .

I am grateful for. . .

Other things that I need to share
with You, God. . .

Amen. Thank You, Father, for hearing my prayers.

"Take courage; I have overcome the world."
John 16:33 nasb

Date:

Dear Heavenly Father,
....
....
....
....

Today, I am feeling anxious about. . .
....
....
....
....
....
....
....
....
....

I confess. . .
....
....
....
....
....
....
....
....
....

I trust that You will. . .
....
....
....
....
....

My soul needs. . .

_____

_____

_____

_____

I am grateful for. . .

_____

_____

_____

_____

Other things that I need to share
with You, God. . .

_____

_____

_____

_____

_____

Amen. Thank You, Father, for hearing my prayers.

*Trust in the LORD with all your heart,
and do not lean on your own understanding.
In all your ways acknowledge him,
and he will make straight your paths.*
PROVERBS 3:5–6 ESV

Date: _____

Dear Heavenly Father, ...
....
....
....
....

Today, I am feeling anxious about. . .
....
....
....
....
....
....
....
....
....

I confess. . .
....
....
....
....
....
....
....

I trust that You will. . .
....
....
....
....
....

My soul needs. . .

I am grateful for. . .

Other things that I need to share
with You, God. . .

Amen. Thank You, Father, for hearing my prayers.

We love because he first loved us.
1 JOHN 4:19 ESV

Date:

Dear Heavenly Father,

Today, I am feeling anxious about. . .

I confess. . .

I trust that You will. . .

My soul needs. . .

I am grateful for. . .

Other things that I need to share
with You, God. . .

Amen. Thank You, Father, for hearing my prayers.

I sought the LORD, and he answered me;
he delivered me from all my fears.
PSALM 34:4 NIV

Date:

Dear Heavenly Father,

Today, I am feeling anxious about. . .

I confess. . .

I trust that You will. . .

My soul needs. . .

I am grateful for. . .

Other things that I need to share
with You, God. . .

Amen. Thank You, Father, for hearing my prayers.

Rest in the LORD, and wait patiently for him.
PSALM 37:7 KJV

Date:

Dear Heavenly Father,

Today, I am feeling anxious about. . .

I confess. . .

I trust that You will. . .

My soul needs. . .

I am grateful for. . .

Other things that I need to share with You, God. . .

Amen. Thank You, Father, for hearing my prayers.

Jesus doesn't change—yesterday, today,
tomorrow, he's always totally himself.
HEBREWS 13:8 MSG

Date:

Dear Heavenly Father,
....
....
....
....
....

Today, I am feeling anxious about. . .
....
....
....
....
....
....
....
....
....

I confess. . .
....
....
....
....
....
....
....
....

I trust that You will. . .
....
....
....
....
....

My soul needs. . .

_____

_____

_____

_____

_____

I am grateful for. . .

_____

_____

_____

_____

Other things that I need to share
with You, God. . .

_____

_____

_____

_____

_____

Amen. Thank You, Father, for hearing my prayers.

Let everything that has breath praise the LORD.
PSALM 150:6 NIV

Date:

Dear Heavenly Father,
....
....
....
....

Today, I am feeling anxious about. . .
....
....
....
....
....
....
....
....
....
....

I confess. . .
....
....
....
....
....
....
....
....
....

I trust that You will. . .
....
....
....
....
....

My soul needs. . .

I am grateful for. . .

Other things that I need to share
with You, God. . .

Amen. Thank You, Father, for hearing my prayers.

_Let us therefore come boldly unto the
throne of grace, that we may obtain mercy,
and find grace to help in time of need._
HEBREWS 4:16 KJV

Date:

Dear Heavenly Father,
....
....
....
....
....

Today, I am feeling anxious about. . .
....
....
....
....
....
....
....
....

I confess. . .
....
....
....
....
....
....
....
....

I trust that You will. . .
....
....
....
....
....

My soul needs. . .

I am grateful for. . .

Other things that I need to share
with You, God. . .

Amen. Thank You, Father, for hearing my prayers.

*"My grace is sufficient for you, for my
power is made perfect in weakness."*
2 CORINTHIANS 12:9 NIV

Date:

Dear Heavenly Father,
....
....
....
....
....

Today, I am feeling anxious about. . .
....
....
....
....
....
....
....
....
....

I confess. . .
....
....
....
....
....
....
....
....

I trust that You will. . .
....
....
....
....
....

My soul needs. . .

I am grateful for. . .

Other things that I need to share with You, God. . .

Amen. Thank You, Father, for hearing my prayers.

If God is for us, who is against us?
ROMANS 8:31 NASB

Date:

Dear Heavenly Father,
....
....
....
....

Today, I am feeling anxious about. . .
....
....
....
....
....
....
....
....
....

I confess. . .
....
....
....
....
....
....
....
....

I trust that You will. . .
....
....
....
....
....

My soul needs. . .

I am grateful for. . .

Other things that I need to share with You, God. . .

Amen. Thank You, Father, for hearing my prayers.

"Everything is possible for one who believes."
MARK 9:23 NIV

Date:

Dear Heavenly Father,

Today, I am feeling anxious about. . .

I confess. . .

I trust that You will. . .

My soul needs. . .

I am grateful for. . .

Other things that I need to share
with You, God. . .

Amen. Thank You, Father, for hearing my prayers.

*In God I have put my trust, I shall not
be afraid. What can man do to me?*
PSALM 56:11 NASB

Date:

Dear Heavenly Father,
....
....
....
....
....

Today, I am feeling anxious about. . .
....
....
....
....
....
....
....
....
....
....

I confess. . .
....
....
....
....
....
....
....
....

I trust that You will. . .
....
....
....
....
....

My soul needs. . .

I am grateful for. . .

Other things that I need to share
with You, God. . .

Amen. Thank You, Father, for hearing my prayers.

"I will trust, and will not be afraid; for the
LORD GOD is my strength and my song,
and he has become my salvation."
ISAIAH 12:2 ESV

Date:

Dear Heavenly Father,

Today, I am feeling anxious about. . .

I confess. . .

I trust that You will. . .

My soul needs. . .

I am grateful for. . .

Other things that I need to share with You, God. . .

Amen. Thank You, Father, for hearing my prayers.

Thou wilt keep him in perfect peace, whose mind is stayed on thee: because he trusteth in thee.
ISAIAH 26:3 KJV

Date:

Dear Heavenly Father,

Today, I am feeling anxious about. . .

I confess. . .

I trust that You will. . .

My soul needs. . .

I am grateful for. . .

Other things that I need to share
with You, God. . .

Amen. Thank You, Father, for hearing my prayers.

*In all things God works for the
good of those who love him.*
ROMANS 8:28 NIV

Date:

Dear Heavenly Father,
....
....
....
....
....

Today, I am feeling anxious about. . .
....
....
....
....
....
....
....
....
....

I confess. . .
....
....
....
....
....
....
....
....

I trust that You will. . .
....
....
....
....
....

My soul needs. . .

I am grateful for. . .

Other things that I need to share with You, God. . .

Amen. Thank You, Father, for hearing my prayers.

Thanks be to God, who gives us the victory through our Lord Jesus Christ.
1 CORINTHIANS 15:57 NASB

Date: ....

Dear Heavenly Father, ...
....
....
....
....

Today, I am feeling anxious about. . .
....
....
....
....
....
....
....
....
....
....

I confess. . .
....
....
....
....
....
....
....
....

I trust that You will. . .
....
....
....
....
....

My soul needs. . .

I am grateful for. . .

Other things that I need to share with You, God. . .

Amen. Thank You, Father, for hearing my prayers.

Weeping may tarry for the night,
but joy comes with the morning.
PSALM 30:5 ESV

Date:

Dear Heavenly Father,...
....
....
....
....

Today, I am feeling anxious about. . .
....
....
....

I confess. . .
....
....
....
....
....
....
....
....

I trust that You will. . .
....
....
....
....
....

My soul needs. . .

....
....
....
....
....

I am grateful for. . .

....
....
....
....

Other things that I need to share
with You, God. . .

....
....
....
....
....

Amen. Thank You, Father, for hearing my prayers.

He has sent me. . .a garment of praise
instead of a spirit of despair.
ISAIAH 61:1, 3 NIV

Date:

Dear Heavenly Father,..
....
....
....
....

Today, I am feeling anxious about. . .
....
....
....
....
....
....
....
....
....

I confess. . .
....
....
....
....
....
....
....
....
....

I trust that You will. . .
....
....
....
....
....

My soul needs. . .

I am grateful for. . .

Other things that I need to share with You, God. . .

Amen. Thank You, Father, for hearing my prayers.

I can do all this through him
who gives me strength.
PHILIPPIANS 4:13 NIV

Date:

Dear Heavenly Father,
....
....
....
....

Today, I am feeling anxious about. . .
....
....
....
....
....
....
....
....
....
....

I confess. . .
....
....
....
....
....
....
....
....
....

I trust that You will. . .
....
....
....
....
....

My soul needs. . .

I am grateful for. . .

Other things that I need to share
with You, God. . .

Amen. Thank You, Father, for hearing my prayers.

_Listen to my prayer, O God,
do not ignore my plea._
PSALM 55:1 NIV

Date:

Dear Heavenly Father,
....
....
....
....

Today, I am feeling anxious about. . .
....
....
....
....
....
....
....
....
....
....

I confess. . .
....
....
....
....
....
....
....
....

I trust that You will. . .
....
....
....
....
....

My soul needs. . .

I am grateful for. . .

Other things that I need to share
with You, God. . .

Amen. Thank You, Father, for hearing my prayers.

O Lord, You have searched me and known me.
PSALM 139:1 NASB

Date:

Dear Heavenly Father,
....
....
....
....
....

Today, I am feeling anxious about. . .
....
....
....
....
....
....
....
....
....

I confess. . .
....
....
....
....
....
....
....
....
....

I trust that You will. . .
....
....
....
....
....

My soul needs. . .

I am grateful for. . .

Other things that I need to share
with You, God. . .

Amen. Thank You, Father, for hearing my prayers.

"For I know the plans I have for you," says the LORD.
"They are plans for good and not for disaster,
to give you a future and a hope."
JEREMIAH 29:11 NLT

📅 Date:

Dear Heavenly Father, ...
....
....
....
....

Today, I am feeling anxious about. . .
....
....
....
....
....
....
....
....
....
....

I confess. . .
....
....
....
....
....
....
....
....
....

I trust that You will. . .
....
....
....
....
....

My soul needs. . .

I am grateful for. . .

Other things that I need to share
with You, God. . .

Amen. Thank You, Father, for hearing my prayers.

Now faith is the assurance of things hoped for,
the conviction of things not seen.
HEBREWS 11:1 ESV

Date:

Dear Heavenly Father,

Today, I am feeling anxious about. . .

I confess. . .

I trust that You will. . .

My soul needs. . .

I am grateful for. . .

Other things that I need to share
with You, God. . .

Amen. Thank You, Father, for hearing my prayers.

Rejoicing in hope, persevering
in tribulation, devoted to prayer.
ROMANS 12:12 NASB

Date:

Dear Heavenly Father,
....
....
....
....
....

Today, I am feeling anxious
about. . .
....
....
....
....
....
....
....
....
....
....

I confess. . .
....
....
....
....
....
....
....
....

I trust that You will. . .
....
....
....
....
....

My soul needs. . .

I am grateful for. . .

Other things that I need to share with You, God. . .

Amen. Thank You, Father, for hearing my prayers.

*I will praise you as long as I live,
lifting up my hands to you in prayer.*
PSALM 63:4 NLT

Date:

Dear Heavenly Father,

Today, I am feeling anxious about. . .

I confess. . .

I trust that You will. . .

My soul needs. . .

I am grateful for. . .

Other things that I need to share with You, God. . .

Amen. Thank You, Father, for hearing my prayers.

Pray like this: Our Father in heaven,
may your name be kept holy.
MATTHEW 6:9 NLT

Date: ....

Dear Heavenly Father, ...
....
....
....
....

Today, I am feeling anxious about. . .

....
....
....
....
....
....
....
....
....

I confess. . .

....
....
....
....
....
....
....
....

I trust that You will. . .

....
....
....
....
....

My soul needs. . .

_____
_____
_____
_____

I am grateful for. . .

_____
_____
_____
_____

Other things that I need to share
with You, God. . .

_____
_____
_____
_____
_____

Amen. Thank You, Father, for hearing my prayers.

*In my distress I called to the LORD. . . . He heard my
voice; my cry came before him, into his ears.*
PSALM 18:6 NIV

Date:

Dear Heavenly Father,
....
....
....
....

Today, I am feeling anxious about. . .
....
....
....
....
....
....
....
....
....

I confess. . .
....
....
....
....
....
....
....
....

I trust that You will. . .
....
....
....
....
....

My soul needs. . .

I am grateful for. . .

Other things that I need to share with You, God. . .

Amen. Thank You, Father, for hearing my prayers.

As soon as I pray, you answer me;
you encourage me by giving me strength.
PSALM 138:3 NLT

Date:

Dear Heavenly Father,
....
....
....
....

Today, I am feeling anxious about. . .
....
....
....
....
....
....
....
....
....
....
....
....

I confess. . .
....
....
....
....
....
....
....
....
....

I trust that You will. . .
....
....
....
....
....

My soul needs. . .

I am grateful for. . .

Other things that I need to share
with You, God. . .

Amen. Thank You, Father, for hearing my prayers.

_[The Lord] will tend his flock like a shepherd;
he will gather the lambs in his arms._
ISAIAH 40:11 ESV

Date:

Dear Heavenly Father,

Today, I am feeling anxious about. . .

I confess. . .

I trust that You will. . .

My soul needs. . .

I am grateful for. . .

Other things that I need to share with You, God. . .

Amen. Thank You, Father, for hearing my prayers.

"Those who hope in me will not be disappointed."
ISAIAH 49:23 NIV

Date:

Dear Heavenly Father,

Today, I am feeling anxious about. . .

I confess. . .

I trust that You will. . .

My soul needs. . .

I am grateful for. . .

Other things that I need to share
with You, God. . .

Amen. Thank You, Father, for hearing my prayers.

"I came that they may have life
and have it abundantly."
JOHN 10:10 ESV

Date:

Dear Heavenly Father,

Today, I am feeling anxious about. . .

I confess. . .

I trust that You will. . .

My soul needs. . .

I am grateful for. . .

Other things that I need to share
with You, God. . .

Amen. Thank You, Father, for hearing my prayers.

*I tell you, you can pray for anything, and if you
believe that you've received it, it will be yours.*
MARK 11:24 NLT

Date:

Dear Heavenly Father,

Today, I am feeling anxious about. . .

I confess. . .

I trust that You will. . .

My soul needs. . .

I am grateful for. . .

Other things that I need to share
with You, God. . .

Amen. Thank You, Father, for hearing my prayers.

_Are any of you suffering hardships? You should pray.
Are any of you happy? You should sing praises._

JAMES 5:13 NLT

Date:

Dear Heavenly Father,
....
....
....
....

Today, I am feeling anxious about. . .
....
....
....
....
....
....
....
....
....

I confess. . .
....
....
....
....
....
....
....
....
....

I trust that You will. . .
....
....
....
....
....

My soul needs. . .

I am grateful for. . .

Other things that I need to share with You, God. . .

Amen. Thank You, Father, for hearing my prayers.

I pray to you, O LORD. I say, "You are my place of refuge. You are all I really want in life."
PSALM 142:5 NLT

Date:

Dear Heavenly Father,
....
....
....
....
....

Today, I am feeling anxious about. . .
....
....
....
....
....
....
....
....
....
....

I confess. . .
....
....
....
....
....
....
....
....

I trust that You will. . .
....
....
....
....
....

My soul needs. . .

I am grateful for. . .

Other things that I need to share
with You, God. . .

Amen. Thank You, Father, for hearing my prayers.

Create in me a pure heart, O God,
and renew a steadfast spirit within me.
PSALM 51:10 NIV

Date:

Dear Heavenly Father,

....
....
....
....

Today, I am feeling anxious about. . .

....
....
....
....
....
....
....
....
....

I confess. . .

....
....
....
....
....
....
....
....
....
....

I trust that You will. . .

....
....
....
....
....

My soul needs. . .

I am grateful for. . .

Other things that I need to share
with You, God. . .

Amen. Thank You, Father, for hearing my prayers.

If we are faithful to the end, trusting God
just as firmly as when we first believed,
we will share in all that belongs to Christ.
HEBREWS 3:14 NLT

Date:

Dear Heavenly Father, ...
....
....
....
....

Today, I am feeling anxious about. . .
....
....
....
....
....
....
....
....
....

I confess. . .
....
....
....
....
....
....
....
....

I trust that You will. . .
....
....
....
....
....

My soul needs. . .

I am grateful for. . .

Other things that I need to share with You, God. . .

Amen. Thank You, Father, for hearing my prayers.

The LORD. . .delights in the prayers of the upright.
PROVERBS 15:8 NLT

Date:

Dear Heavenly Father,
....
....
....
....
....

Today, I am feeling anxious about. . .
....
....
....
....
....
....
....
....
....

I confess. . .
....
....
....
....
....
....
....
....

I trust that You will. . .
....
....
....
....
....

My soul needs. . .

I am grateful for. . .

Other things that I need to share with You, God. . .

Amen. Thank You, Father, for hearing my prayers.

The LORD is good to those who wait for him,
to the soul who seeks him.
LAMENTATIONS 3:25 ESV

Date:

Dear Heavenly Father,
....
....
....
....

Today, I am feeling anxious about. . .
....
....
....
....
....
....
....
....

I confess. . .
....
....
....
....
....
....
....
....

I trust that You will. . .
....
....
....
....
....

My soul needs. . .

I am grateful for. . .

Other things that I need to share
with You, God. . .

Amen. Thank You, Father, for hearing my prayers.

_I will sing to the LORD, because He
has dealt bountifully with me._
PSALM 13:6 NASB

Date:

Dear Heavenly Father,
....
....
....
....

Today, I am feeling anxious about. . .
....
....
....
....
....
....
....
....

I confess. . .
....
....
....
....
....
....
....

I trust that You will. . .
....
....
....
....
....

My soul needs. . .

I am grateful for. . .

Other things that I need to share
with You, God. . .

Amen. Thank You, Father, for hearing my prayers.

*The Word became flesh and dwelt among us,
and we have seen his glory, glory as of the only
Son from the Father, full of grace and truth.*
JOHN 1:14 ESV

Date:

Dear Heavenly Father,

Today, I am feeling anxious about. . .

I confess. . .

I trust that You will. . .

My soul needs. . .

I am grateful for. . .

Other things that I need to share with You, God. . .

Amen. Thank You, Father, for hearing my prayers.

"As the heavens are higher than the earth, so are my ways higher than your ways and my thoughts than your thoughts."
ISAIAH 55:9 NIV

Date:

Dear Heavenly Father,

....
....
....
....

Today, I am feeling anxious about. . .

....
....
....
....
....
....
....
....

I confess. . .

....
....
....
....
....
....
....
....

I trust that You will. . .

....
....
....
....
....

My soul needs. . .

I am grateful for. . .

Other things that I need to share
with You, God. . .

Amen. Thank You, Father, for hearing my prayers.

But I'm in the very presence of God—
oh, how refreshing it is!
PSALM 73:27 MSG

Date:

Dear Heavenly Father,...
....
....
....
....

Today, I am feeling anxious about. . .
....
....
....

I confess. . .
....
....
....
....
....
....
....
....
....
....

I trust that You will. . .
....
....
....
....
....

My soul needs. . .

I am grateful for. . .

Other things that I need to share with You, God. . .

Amen. Thank You, Father, for hearing my prayers.

Let your unfailing love surround us,
LORD, for our hope is in you alone.
PSALM 33:22 NLT

Date:

Dear Heavenly Father,
....
....
....
....

Today, I am feeling anxious about. . .
....
....
....
....
....
....
....
....
....
....

I confess. . .
....
....
....
....
....
....
....
....

I trust that You will. . .
....
....
....
....
....

My soul needs. . .

I am grateful for. . .

Other things that I need to share
with You, God. . .

Amen. Thank You, Father, for hearing my prayers.

Search me, O God, and know my heart;
try me and know my anxious thoughts;
and see if there be any hurtful way in me,
and lead me in the everlasting way.
PSALM 139:23–24 NASB

Date:

Dear Heavenly Father, ...
....
....
....
....

Today, I am feeling anxious about. . .
....
....
....
....
....
....
....
....
....

I confess. . .
....
....
....
....
....
....
....
....

I trust that You will. . .
....
....
....
....
....

My soul needs. . .

I am grateful for. . .

Other things that I need to share with You, God. . .

Amen. Thank You, Father, for hearing my prayers.

What does the LORD require of you
but to do justice, and to love kindness,
and to walk humbly with your God?
MICAH 6:8 ESV

Date:

Dear Heavenly Father,

Today, I am feeling anxious about. . .

I confess. . .

I trust that You will. . .

My soul needs. . .

I am grateful for. . .

Other things that I need to share
with You, God. . .

Amen. Thank You, Father, for hearing my prayers.

*"The eyes of the Lord watch over those who
do right, and his ears are open to their prayers."*
1 Peter 3:12 nlt

Date:

Dear Heavenly Father,

Today, I am feeling anxious about. . .

I confess. . .

I trust that You will. . .

My soul needs. . .

I am grateful for. . .

Other things that I need to share
with You, God. . .

Amen. Thank You, Father, for hearing my prayers.

*But when you pray, go away by yourself,
shut the door behind you, and pray to your
Father in private. Then your Father, who
sees everything, will reward you.*

MATTHEW 6:6 NLT

Date:

Dear Heavenly Father,

Today, I am feeling anxious about. . .

I confess. . .

I trust that You will. . .

My soul needs. . .

I am grateful for. . .

Other things that I need to share
with You, God. . .

Amen. Thank You, Father, for hearing my prayers.

*"You will go out in joy and be led
forth in peace; the mountains and hills
will burst into song before you."*
ISAIAH 55:12 NIV

Date:

Dear Heavenly Father,
....
....
....
....
....

Today, I am feeling anxious about. . .
....
....
....
....
....
....
....
....

I confess. . .
....
....
....
....
....
....
....
....

I trust that You will. . .
....
....
....
....
....

My soul needs. . .

I am grateful for. . .

Other things that I need to share
with You, God. . .

Amen. Thank You, Father, for hearing my prayers.

Hallelujah! O my soul, praise God!
All my life long I'll praise God, singing
songs to my God as long as I live.
PSALM 146:1–2 MSG

Date:

Dear Heavenly Father, ...
....
....
....
....

Today, I am feeling anxious about. . .

....
....
....
....
....
....
....
....
....

I confess. . .

....
....
....
....
....
....
....
....

I trust that You will. . .

....
....
....
....
....

My soul needs. . .

I am grateful for. . .

Other things that I need to share
with You, God. . .

Amen. Thank You, Father, for hearing my prayers.

*When doubts filled my mind, your comfort
gave me renewed hope and cheer.*
PSALM 94:19 NLT

Date:

Dear Heavenly Father,
....
....
....
....

Today, I am feeling anxious about. . .
....
....
....
....
....
....
....
....
....

I confess. . .
....
....
....
....
....
....
....
....
....

I trust that You will. . .
....
....
....
....
....

My soul needs. . .

I am grateful for. . .

Other things that I need to share with You, God. . .

Amen. Thank You, Father, for hearing my prayers.

I am counting on the LORD;
yes, I am counting on him.
PSALM 130:5 NLT

Date:

Dear Heavenly Father, ...
....
....
....
....

Today, I am feeling anxious about. . .
....
....
....
....
....
....
....
....
....

I confess. . .
....
....
....
....
....
....
....
....

I trust that You will. . .
....
....
....
....
....

My soul needs. . .

I am grateful for. . .

Other things that I need to share with You, God. . .

Amen. Thank You, Father, for hearing my prayers.

*"No one who trusts God like this—
heart and soul—will ever regret it."*
ROMANS 10:11 MSG

Date:

Dear Heavenly Father,
....
....
....
....

Today, I am feeling anxious about. . .
....
....
....
....
....
....
....
....

I confess. . .
....
....
....
....
....
....
....
....

I trust that You will. . .
....
....
....
....
....

My soul needs. . .

I am grateful for. . .

Other things that I need to share
with You, God. . .

Amen. Thank You, Father, for hearing my prayers.

The hopes of the godly result in happiness.
PROVERBS 10:28 NLT

Date:

Dear Heavenly Father,
....
....
....
....

Today, I am feeling anxious about. . .
....
....
....
....
....
....
....
....
....
....

I confess. . .
....
....
....
....
....
....
....
....
....

I trust that You will. . .
....
....
....
....
....

My soul needs. . .

I am grateful for. . .

Other things that I need to share
with You, God. . .

Amen. Thank You, Father, for hearing my prayers.

I have been young and now I am old,
yet I have not seen the righteous forsaken
or his descendants begging bread.
PSALM 37:25 NASB

Date: ....

Dear Heavenly Father, ...
....
....
....
....

Today, I am feeling anxious about. . .
....
....
....

I confess. . .
....
....
....
....
....
....
....
....

I trust that You will. . .
....
....
....
....
....

My soul needs. . .

I am grateful for. . .

Other things that I need to share with You, God. . .

Amen. Thank You, Father, for hearing my prayers.

You're my place of quiet retreat;
I wait for your Word to renew me.
PSALM 119:114 MSG

Date: _____

Dear Heavenly Father, _____
....
....
....
....

Today, I am feeling anxious about. . .
....
....
....
....
....
....
....
....
....
....
....

I confess. . .
....
....
....
....
....
....
....
....
....

I trust that You will. . .
....
....
....
....
....

My soul needs. . .

I am grateful for. . .

Other things that I need to share
with You, God. . .

Amen. Thank You, Father, for hearing my prayers.

*Delight yourself in the LORD; and He
will give you the desires of your heart.*
PSALM 37:4 NASB

Date: ....

Dear Heavenly Father, ...
....
....
....
....

Today, I am feeling anxious about. . .
....
....
....
....
....
....
....
....

I confess. . .
....
....
....
....
....
....
....
....

I trust that You will. . .
....
....
....
....
....

My soul needs...

I am grateful for...

Other things that I need to share with You, God...

Amen. Thank You, Father, for hearing my prayers.

A joyful heart is good medicine.
PROVERBS 17:22 ESV

Date:

Dear Heavenly Father,

....
....
....
....

Today, I am feeling anxious about. . .

....
....
....
....
....
....
....
....
....

I confess. . .

....
....
....
....
....
....
....
....
....

I trust that You will. . .

....
....
....
....
....

My soul needs. . .

I am grateful for. . .

Other things that I need to share
with You, God. . .

Amen. Thank You, Father, for hearing my prayers.

*I pray that your hearts will be flooded with
light so that you can understand the confident
hope he has given to those he called.*
EPHESIANS 1:18 NLT

Date:

Dear Heavenly Father,
....
....
....
....
....

Today, I am feeling anxious about. . .
....
....
....
....
....
....
....
....
....
....

I confess. . .
....
....
....
....
....
....
....
....

I trust that You will. . .
....
....
....
....
....

My soul needs. . .

I am grateful for. . .

Other things that I need to share
with You, God. . .

Amen. Thank You, Father, for hearing my prayers.

Answer me when I call to you, O God.
PSALM 4:1 NLT

Date:

Dear Heavenly Father,

....

....

....

....

Today, I am feeling anxious about...

....

....

....

....

....

....

....

....

....

I confess...

....

....

....

....

....

....

....

....

I trust that You will...

....

....

....

....

....

My soul needs. . .

I am grateful for. . .

Other things that I need to share
with You, God. . .

Amen. Thank You, Father, for hearing my prayers.

_"Blessed is the man who trusts in the
LORD and whose trust is the LORD."_
JEREMIAH 17:7 NASB

Date:

Dear Heavenly Father,
....
....
....
....
....

Today, I am feeling anxious
about. . .
....
....
....
....
....
....
....
....

I confess. . .
....
....
....
....
....
....
....
....

I trust that You will. . .
....
....
....
....
....